Northside Poetry

by
Tone One

Writers Club Press

San Jose · New York · Lincoln · Shanghai

Northside Poetry
Copyright © 1999 by Anthony Matos

ISBN: 1-893652-56-4

Published by Writer's Club Press, an imprint of iUniverse.com, Inc.

iUniverse.com, Inc.
620 North 48th Street
Suite 201
Lincoln NE 68504-3467
www.iuniverse.com

URL: http://www.writersclub.com

TO THE WOMAN
WHO GAVE ME LIFE,
AND TO THE WOMAN
WHO SAVED MY LIFE
I LOVE YOU BOTH!

CONTENTS

Chapter 1

3 HOURS OF 2 DAYS

We looked into each other's eyes
And all I see is your soul crying for life.
So I hugged you and I can feel your soul,
You're so cold inside.
"Thank you!
Thank you for being there with and
For me," I said.
A grateful emotion feeling I've released.
You gave me 3 hours of 2 days of your life.
And I gave you my feelings, my reasons, and my
Thoughts to you.
Each spot I touched you,
You quivered.
Each spot I kissed you,
You moaned.
Tell me! Tell me out loud.
Who do you see?
A man, a soldier, or just a lover?
"A man by day,
A soldier by night,
And a lover for 3 hours of 2 days," she said.

SAY MY NAME

Sensation which I can't explain!
A beauty which is always still and the same!
This amour will last forever.
And I worship the ground you walk on!
I need you and you're my every breath.
You touch me with enjoyment of power.
Sinless which you have within yourself.
Slowly I kiss you on your chest
With a strong amorous feeling.
Sexy if what you are!
Sexy is when you're laying warm and naked at
My side.
A sensation which I can't explain!
A beauty which is only you,
My love, my angel, my Antonia.
And you end the game with a name!
"Baby! O, Tony!"

A VOICE FROM A BASTARD!

There is so much mentally unbalance pain for you!
You denied me of my living and dying ways.
You were once there but now you're gone.
Remembering only when you're next to me
Until I forgotten that you left me,
Isn't what a boy's life should be!
You subside yourself down
And made your own family!
But where do I stand?
Or
When do I speak my mind?
I stare into your brown eyes
And I see it clearly!
The brown-eyed man with three kids.
But it's okay!
You're my personal problem, not them!
And I taste the jealousy in your
Wife's presence when I stand on
Your doorsteps at home.
You left me with my hands dirty!
But why did you treat me like shit?
All you are is a selfish and stupid man.
I was born as a bastard,
And will die as one!
Hoping that you die in my bloodshed
I can only pray.
You deserve every pain and sorrow in hell,
As well as the burns and torment you have given me!
The best punishment as a gift you have given me
Is being a fucking bastard!
So let me be,
And die in peace!
(Without you!)

MY TEACHER, MY IN-LAW

There were thousands of words
I needed to tell you.
But you're not listening.
So many ways of expressions to you.
But you can't see me.
A room where you slept in and mope in,
Is now silent.
(Not even the inhale of your cigarettes, when lit)
Sorry to hear of you sleeping and never waking up!
Once a person dies,
A child is born.
They used to say to me.
I don't know if I should feel disappointed,
Or be satisfied of your death.
But you made room for a new child.
All know is I'll miss you!
I don't hate you,
(But then again)
I don't love you.
I was just glad of knowing you were there.
Awake or sleeping—you were there.
I won't reject God for his doing!
'Cause I understand his job!
(It took me a while!)
But I understand it now.
And with a grateful appreciation,
I thank you for having me feel
What your only child felt.
A great feeling of sorrow!
And with that,
You give me another look at family gathering!
You laughed at everything in your path.
Nature threw problems at your feet,
And you just laughed.
I guess your death is greatly funny,
"Cause you laughed at that also!
From life to death,
From health to sickness,
You've proven to me,

That you are better than I am.
'Cause you're with Mr. Number One (GOD)
And you finally found peace!

INSANITY IN THE FIRST DEGREE!

Look at my sorry soul,
And tell me what do you see?
Do you see a man or a beast?
Or just both of us,
Trapped in a hopeless state of mind?
From a juvenile to a full grown man,
But that alone isn't enough!
Wanting to know if I follow the light,
Where would it take me?
Wanting to know is there real life after death.
(I won't know until I get there!)
The child inside me wants to stop the madness.
But the beast outside of me
Wants to continue the war and destroy us all.
Sitting on the floor with a gun in my mouth,
Will stop the war inside me.
Or maybe the childhood wounds!
Because it's taking forever to heal.
I'll hear no more of my brother or sisters.
I'll hear no more calling!
"Bastard!" "Motherfucker!" she says.
Or *"Stupid!" "Asshole,"* he says
It will be no more words!
(Just peace!)
Hoping and wishing for a comfort
In my boneless, soul of mine.
I sit on my floor, with a tear on my face.
And crazy things pop into my mind.
Screaming from the top of my lungs
Dangerously and say to myself
"If you're going to do it, so then do it,
You fool!"

CHECKMATE!

I walked towards you,
As you lay across the floor clothesless.
I stand over you wondering if this is right.
Right or wrong it's going to happen.
So I lower myself to your level.
"Play me like the bitch I am!"
You said
So I will play!
I played, licked sucked, ate, teased
Sticked and wet every moment of you
On the cold hard floor.
And I whisper in your ear,
With a satisfaction
"Checkmate!"
I sat up and a hole appears on my chest.
Released the joy and relaxation
Hell was holding back from me,
And it feels so good.
You looked at me with the sensation
Experience at the peak of sexual
Excitement on your face and whispered,
"Checkmate."
You woke up that morning,
Realizing it was a dream.
You looked to the side of the bed,
And arose with a note!
It said,
"Checkmate my love, it's no dream!"

PARA MARIA

Some day I will realize
The days and nights of passion,
We had been real.
And I played such games with your love.
Regretting the moments,
I walked out your life.
Knowing I'll have worries and sleeplessness
Only breaking my heart into pieces,
"I can only scream!"
I have pain in my heart,
And it's tearing me apart
"I've been shot in the chest!" you said.
Dropping to my knees
With you still,
In my arms.
I feel the loneliness over me,
Like if rain is upon me.
I feel so lonely
So lonely
And all I can say is
I love you, I miss you, and I'm sorry!

A LADY TO KILL FOR!

It's one of those hot sticky nights,
Dry and windless.
The kind that makes people does sweaty,
Secret things.
I thought of you when we were together
In a small dark room,
Just holding each other.
I would murder for you
As well as I would die for you!
I'm thinking of all the ways I screwed up,
And what I'd give for one clear chance
To wipe the slate clean.
It's so hard!
To be able to dig my way out of the numb,
Gray hell that is in my life.
Jesus! It's so cold in my soul without her!
As I sit in my car waiting for the green light to change,
I look to the side view mirror,
And say, "I'll give anything just to cut loose,
Just to feel the fire,
One more time!

MY FAITH!

We all have temptations within us.
But mine is much stronger,
Cause my temptations are based on faith,
Full faith.
"No such faith lives in you!" they said.
Knowing I choose to be true.
I am what I am,
A true definition of a man!
I don't play games,
'Cause I'm young at heart.
I'll love you and I'll need your dear love,
You're my true love,
'Cause it's in the soul,
My soul.
To be faithful means nothing to you!
But for this poor soul it means,
True love and true compassion.
There's no kissing or telling,
Or no playing or tricking with the mind of many
Hearts.
'Cause tricks are for the mindless,
Not men who are real at heart.
Real men with real true hearts!

FADING SHADOWS!

Standing inside shadows
I think to myself the madness,
I have stored all these years within myself.
Sweat, running down my face.
I'm running crazy away from it.
Satan watching over me with
A joyful smile on his face!
I hear laughter in the air.
I can't hide! It'll find me!
I don't know where it's coming from.
I'm tired of running from it!
"Face Me!" I yelled.
"You think I'm scared of you?
Stand in my presence!" I yelled demanding.
No one appears before me.
I crouch down to my knees
Waiting for my senses to calm down!
It's no help,
I'm still furious!
I've close my eyes,
It's not helping.
I still feel it clearly!
I feel the scars on my face,
Bleeding from my lips.
I've felt the beating.
Does it ever stop hurting?
It seems that they whipped me
With a leather strip on my back!
Carving names of hatred upon me!
Breaking me down with words.
Jesus!
It hurts more when it heals.
But now I finally stand in front of the mirror,
Bleeding to death.
And say to myself, "I'm a man with bad luck!"
No! It's not bad luck,
It's life and it's willpower.
But yet, but yet, it's glory 'cause it's over!
I look at myself and laugh,

But people who test me wonder why.
They don't see what I see within myself.
Scars cuts, wounds, and embarrassments.
You can't hurt me any longer!
I do more destruction than weeping!
I can still look at you and smile,
As you take your last breath!
Now I'm saying, "Run, motherfucker, Run!"
Now this private confession is over
Finally!

THE SMELL OF GLORY

Freedom, O Freedom
I can taste it,
As if raindrops fell on my tongue.
Staring at a man as he says sermons to me.
No harm done,
Just pure comfort!
The word of God cuts me like a razor,
(Making my ears bleed)
Cutting out the loneliness
Out of my dark heart and soul.
Filling the dark skies
Into sunshine and rainbows.
I know more today,
Then,
I knew yesterday.
I know that today,
I did do wrong.
Satan will never have the best of me.
For even if I'll walk in darkness again,
Jesus is with me!
For better or worse!
Freedom, O Freedom
How sweet it sounds.
I shed tears for you,
And
I shed tears for myself.
But I won't shed tears for hatred.
For the great power of Christ,
And you my Lord almighty,
I can survive.
My dear God! Thank you
For sparing another day of paradise
Your paradise to me.

MY FIRST LADY

I smell the fragrance in the air,
When you pass by me.
Let me listen to your voice,
For it sounds sweet.
Kissing you repeatedly feels so good.
Having you in my arms feels glamorous to me.
Spend the night with me.
So I can give you pure ecstasy.
For every president there is a first lady.
And you are my first and my final lady!
Come and sit next to me.
For you and I can rule the world
That the men of devils in this world created.
I don't ask for your sex,
Just for your thoughts and feelings.
There's no need for your beauty,
'Cause your love completes that task!
I believe from my heart, mind and soul.
That you and I will live for a thousand years.
Even after life,
I will still always love you.
Let me love you constantly,
'Cause the fragrance from your body,
Makes me want you more.
Let me listen to your voice
For your voice is sweet as your light-skinned face.
Let me drop down to my knees
And lay my head against your thigh.
Pass your nails slowly across my back
And speak the words that makes you a queen.
Lay warm next to me
And tell me that you love me.
Hold my hand and kiss me when I'm asleep.
Your beauty alone makes my heart quickly beat again.
I'll touch your face and I feel you are content!
Let me kiss your forehead when we make love.
And your know it's always been ecstasy!

YOU'RE ABSOLUTELY SEXY!

The way you stand,
Or the way you walk.
Maybe it's your lips,
Your soft red lips
Or the way you bite that pencil.
All I know it's absolutely sexy!
The way you talk,
Or the way you sit and fold your legs.
Maybe it's your appearance.
All I know is when you pass your hands
Through your hair,
It's absolutely sexy!
The movement of your tongue passes through your lips
is always a creative imagination!
Let me stare at the body
That makes me quiver!
Constantly!
Let me hold your hands and pull you towards me,
For I can tell what flavor you are.
Let me hold you tightly,
For I can feel the warmth from you.
I love the stare you give me,
I wonder the expectation in your mind.
Kiss me as your lover,
Not as your friend.
And I'll make love to you as a king,
Not as a husband!
My dear young lady!
('Cause we are all young in the vision of love.)
Do you need me?
Will you let me grab you?
And kiss you repeatedly?
'Cause the way you stand
Or the way you walk
It just makes me want to make love to you
On a bed filled with rose petals
in the middle of a thunderstorm!
And you are absolutely,
No questions asked
Sexy!

THE SPANISH VALENTINE

So many ways in telling you,
I love you.
You fulfill my every breath
With your rose scented body.
I can touch and feel your body in my dreams.
I can taste your sweat in my mouth.
I love the movement of your lips
When you say my name.
Come into my arms and let me hold you.
Let me make love to you repeatedly,
Throughout the night!
Lay your head against my chest,
And listen to the drums of my Latino heart.
Close your eyes and I'll whisper
Sweet poetry in your ears.
I can tell in your hungry eyes,
It's been a long time!
And I will love you longer.
Let me make you quiver,
And say things you never said before.
Say my name and I'll give you
Pleasant pleasure that lasts a lifetime.
Tell me that you'll stay with me,
And you'll never leave my side.
My love for you,
It will always be.
My temperature rises when
I'm next or around you.
My love for you is quickly, magically growing.
And I believe that this casual affair
Will so turn to love.
Give me your time and I'll feed you
Love that never dies.
I'll promise Valentine's Day everyday
For your entire life.
If you offer my world your love,
I'll give you faithful, sinless passion!
Let me fill the empty spaces
On your body with my breath and touch.

Let our bodies rub against each other,
For our hearts can burn eternally.
And in my dreams I've kissed you
A million times
And when I close my eyes,
I see you standing before me.
O love, my love
I've never missed one night
Of my dreams without you.
I have prayed for your touch.
I never knew a man to love like this.
It feels so huge or just strong.
It tastes so sweet,
Ever so sweet!
You alone comfort me with your beauty.

LETTERS FROM MY LIPS

Every night when I'm staring at the top of my ceiling.
I get this crumble sweet thought,
But I never knew the meaning of,
Why!
Why you hypnotize me in such a way?
Tears in my eyes,
As the moon light fades,
I can't hold you,
I can't kiss you,
'Cause you're so far away,
So all I do is miss you.
But when I stare at your picture,
I feel I'm with you,
From the moments and the words
I used to whisper in your earlobe.
And there on,
I hope we can last forever.
And maybe we can be as one!
That's why I wrote this letter,
For I can tell you,
The way I feel is real and it's unlimited.
No one will love you the way I do!
You turned my useless, clueless days
From thunderstorms to sunshine.
That's why I have to continue to say,
It takes a woman like you.
Silence,
Silence, I can't bare
It you're not here at my tearful side.
I can't express or share,
All of my feelings which are still there.
From a dream I awaken.
I felt heart broken,
Restless nights,
I sweated, just hoping,
That you call me,
And then prepare me.
Don't forget the past,
Don't let me stand- alone.

I needed you most of all.
I'm hanging from a string,
Don't let me fall,
My princess!
I'm going insane
Since the day you left,
It hasn't been the same.
Just give me one more shot at love.
We were made together
Just as flesh and blood.
You're so tender and sweet,
My queen.
It takes a woman like you!

YOUR HEAVEN, MY HELL!

"Look at her and tell me,
What do you see?"
She believes in you,
And worships the ground you walked on.
She changed her ways from sinful to sinless.
You washed her temple down,
With your water...you're holy water!
Your words told her things like
Be good, and don't lie or cheat!
You asked her to be the opposite of me,
So she did,
She's holy and I'm evil.
'Cause I cheat and lie.
I lie to stay painless.
I cheat to survive the world you created!
You told me once on a morning dream:
Wherever you go, I'll always be there,
For and with you.
Yes! I believed you.
But just to fuck things up for me.
You must remember,
We lie like the devil,
Forgetting everything,
Ending in our own being.
One way or another you try to keep me!
Just because you create this temple,
You believe you have the right to crush
Or have the right to perish me for my doing!
Damn you man!
So if you want me that bad,
Let her go.
Let my wife's soul go.
End your lawful ways to my wife's being!
Then you and I can battle as two men.
King of kings
And lord of lords that we are!
And we will see who is weaker and who is stronger.
'Cause I'm tired of you rejecting me
'Cause of your dictates of moral laws.

MY BATTLE WITH LIFE

Sometimes in my life,
I have had dreams.
But not one can match the battle of life.
When I sleep I wonder the places that'll be.
And when my breath changes deep.
I found myself in a world of sand and bloodshed.
And in the center of the sand field,
A man stands there inactive.
He was tall and wore a dark robe,
I couldn't see his face.
(He was covering it away from me)
It seems that he was bald.
He was carrying a long shaft with a sharply
Pointed head in his hand.
And says to me quietly
"At last you arrived,
I thought you weren't coming!"
I asked him, "Where was I? What is this place?"
He reluctant and says
"You are where people go to be judged for their
Doing!
Here, which you can see, is that you are
Trapped in a twenty-four hour glass!
And too leave this place, you must face your
Ugliest secrets! You must face me as a lord just as you say!"
He turns towards me and I froze.
My body tightens;
I felt my heart begin to race,
I couldn't breathe for a second.
His face was horrifying,
He was not human
He was immortal!
Part of his face was there,
But his other half was decomposed, bleeding!
With the shock of his face I whispered,
"You're the reaper."
He yells loudly and slaps me on my chest with
His staff.
Quickly I respond and hit back!

It felt like hours I was fighting with this demon.
He rips my clothes and laughs at me.
He throws his staff at me as if it was a spear.
He was surprised that I caught it.
He grins at me and says,
"What are you going to do with that?"
With a smile that a dog would make.
I said back to him furiously with my chest
Scratched
"I'm going to break it so you can fight
Me as a real man!"
"No, you little fucker!" he said
I raise the staff over my head and placed it down
On my knee and broke it.
It felt like I did something right.
The reaper didn't move towards me.
He just vanished into sand before my eyes.
All was left of him was the dark robe.
And the broken staff.
Quickly I woke up!
And I heard the sounds of birds, cars and people
Laughing outside.
I woke up in a cold sweat.
I got up to the edge of the bed and passed my
Fingers through my hair and walked towards the mirror!
My chest still remained with the scratches
That was no dream I had!
I took a deep breath and said, "I guess I was a lord in both worlds!"

POOR MAN TO A QUEEN

As I stand by my window wondering about you,
I taste the sweet memories.
I don't know the reason of why
You're impressive in such a way.
I beg for your beauty every night of my life.
I try to call you,
But I'm too scared as a newborn child.
So, all I will do is miss you.
I'm only one man but not a rich man.
For your voice and beauty,
Is worth more than this poetry from my heart.
I can't shower you with diamonds or pearls,
But I can rinse you down with the heat of the love
Of my hands passing across you soft, smooth lips.
I can't offer you all the surface of the world
But I can give you the entire core of my heart.
A rich man can earn love with money,
But I would work to earn your love
With these simple words from my heart and soul.

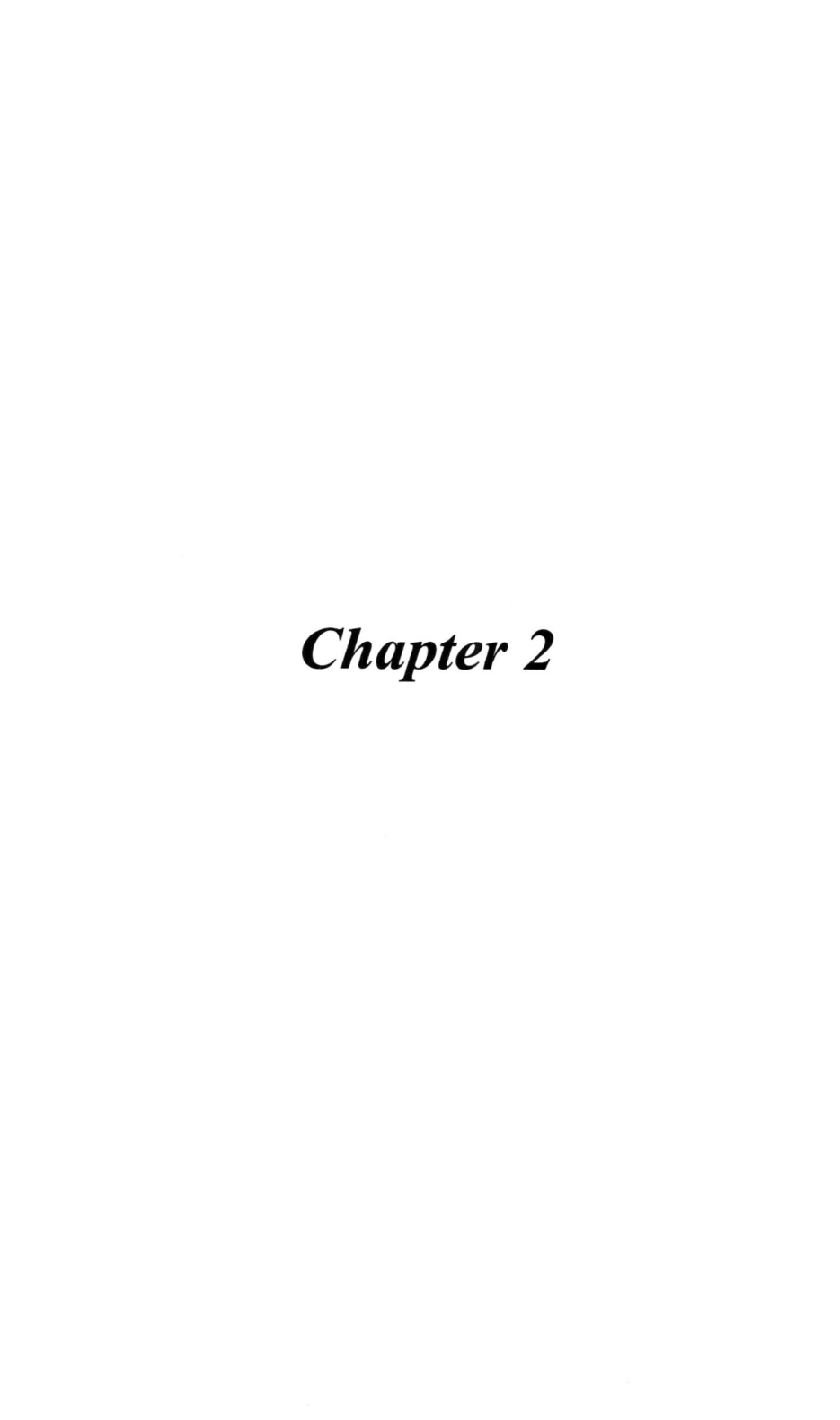

Chapter 2

TO MY PAPA!

You rose me to the top,
If I was a born prince.
You watched me take my first steps.
Where's my hug as a reward?
You kissed me on the forehead when I slept.
But yet I don't feel a thing.
Denied, rejected is what I was!
You said you loved me!
But I don't feel a warm spot within me.
"Mi casa es su casa!"
But yet I need an invitation to see you.
"I'll always be there for you!"
Yet I can't breathe without your permission?
I dropped to my knees,
(I lack the need for love, respect and the need for a father!)
Te busque—
But you're nowhere to be found.
You said if you didn't love me,
I wouldn't have your last name.
Oh father! Dear father!
Love doesn't come from a name,
It's from the heart,
Your heart
I'm your son, your first born son!
Why did I feel so left out?
Don't touch or hold me,
I learn to do without it.
I used to have a role model
But it's just all an illusion.
You promised me compassion, dreams, and understanding.
All you fed me was large lies.
Life was hell to me.
I learned to live with it.
(It's home now)
I walked with pride within myself.
Never crawled to the top!
Started with nothing! I have something now.
I don't need you or your love.
"He's the reason for your success!"

Tone One

(People used to say)
But you're not mine!
Not mine!
As I stand in front of you,
Man-to-man with the Four Corners
Of hell with me.
All I can say is " May we meet in hell again one Day!"

JUST MEMORIES

Let me give you my time,
My love, my passion, and my heart.
Let me touch you in ways no other man has
Touched you before.
Saying your name loudly in my mind,
Still brings back fantasy memories to me!
Time after time,
I craved for your scent and taste.
Remembering the days and nights we slept together.
I still remember the times I laid on the floor,
To eat you alive.
Wondering if I am still your love (even after)
When we made love in the beaches of ecstasy.
What I would just give to do it all again with you.
Let me touch, feel, and kiss every inch of your body!
Pull me towards you,
I know you still love me!
Having you moan and whisper *"Jesus Christ"*
When I pass a simple stroke of my hands across
Your body.
I love when I take you to ecstasy when you say
"Love me like you never loved another!"
Having you stroke back and forth on me,
While I pull your hair.
(I know you loved it!)
As much as you loved me!
But now I hunger for your kiss,
And I'm longing for your touch.
My memories of you are locked forever in a dream.
I know that you will always race through my
Mind,
I know deep in my veins that you will still
Be in my vision when I close my eyes.
"I love you and always will"
You said to me one autumn day.
I believed the words, you told me.
But now that you're gone,
I see things I've gained in time.
You're in heaven now and I'm still alive and well.

Tone One

I know that you watched over me with angels and God.
Since then I've loved you with all my heart
But
The memory of you still remains.
And that's all what will remain!
Are your memories,
And just your memories!

EXISTENCE IN MY MIND

I can see you as if you were standing here with me.
I wonder and crave for your emotions!
The taste of your remains is still there.
And the fragrance of your body is still on my
Hands.
Remembering the time I held and walked with
You in my mind.
Needing to know if you were thinking
Or thought of me in your dreams,
Time after time.
I've missed you as much as I've loved you.
Waking up in the darkness,
Yelling your name in my mind.
Reaching for your touch,
I felt the breeze
Of your memories on my fingertips.
Wishing for my eyes to stay closed for I,
Can only see your beauty in my head.
Cutting out my tongue for I can only,
Remember the taste of your body's wetness
In my mouth.
O my sweet candy apple,
How much I love simply looking at you.
'Cause your face and walk brings a child
Out of me.
I have felt your heart as well as you felt mine.
You're soft as a pillow and I'm hard as steel.
Your voice was simple as silk,
But my poetry to a woman trapped in my mind
Is not equal to the requirements of your voice.
But when one day my dream will becomes a reality,
That will be the day that I'll take my final breath and say
"I love you,
And farewell my love"
"Farewell my handsome prince,
For it was always a reality!"
She said back at me.

2 HUNDRED YEARS

Waiting and waiting
I just can't wait.

SERVANT: *Relax, my lord!!*

I have waited for over 2 hundred years,
And today I have the chance to breathe
So much easier than yesterday!

SERVANT: *Relax, my lord! Just relax*!

That's the woman I've seen in my past
Life and in my dreams.
I refuse to let her go!
Not like that,
Not today, not ever

.

SERVANT: *How do you know what she wants?*
Have you read her thoughts?
My lord good things come to those who wait.

I stand by her and I sweat,
I stare into your eyes,
And I cannot control my heart from beating slower.

SERVANT: *You have planned your time for2 hundred years,*
And I can see that you will out live all of us.
But one day you must understand,
you shall exit this world also!

I will crush those who stand in front or behind me.
To just have her,
My love for just one more night.
For I am older, stronger and wiser than them,
Or those who dare declare war on my life!

SERVANT: *I trust your judgment my lord*
For you have eliminated hate all around you.
So then go my lord and take the love

Your heart desires for
And live for another 2 hundred years!

MEMORIES OF YOU

Everynight I sleep in my bed
And I see you in my dreams.
I see you playing the piano on the gateway of my heaven.
O how beautiful you look in white.
I remember the mornings you called me
Just to tell me that you loved me.
In my mind and heart,
I shed tears long before you.
I remember the times you and I spoke,
Alone together sharing our thoughts and reasons.
Never once did you back off.
Never once did you cry to me,
But towards me.
I know you loved me.
I would bury a mountain to bits for you.
I'm a man who will fight against not some
But all odds for you.
I myself can't bring the power within me
To bring you back into my arms again.
You gave me an offer that I couldn't refuse,
I did refuse!
Yes! I do still love you but my life
Means more to me than life itself.
I will stand in front of lightening for you.
I'll yell your name until you can hear me.
I'll cry until you wipe your hands across
My face and say
"I am here for and with you forever".
And for you, I'll bury one million of people
In just one word of your name.
Crush those who dare come between
You and I in my dream or reality.
Because all I have is memories,
Of you and I making love in the morning.
Kissing each other with passion as
Children would play games in the evening.
O, my dear Lord give me the strength
To tell her that I will never live again
As I was living with her!

SLIPPING BY

Come into my arms
And let me embrace you tight.
Let me be the love
To make love to you throughout the midnight hour.
Could it be that my love
Has made my feelings appear clearly.
You promised me "Mi amour"
That you'll never let me go.
Don't ever leave,
Don't ever go away.
I'll promise to you "Mi amour"
My love for you will always be here.
Please don't ever leave me,
'Cause my love for you is strong.
I love you, I always need you,
Your always on my mind,
And I refuse to let you go.
You once told me on a line,
That you was always be by my side
I looked in both directions,
"I can't see you"
You're gone.
I put all my tears in a clear bottle,
Just to remember the little things we did together.
But if my bottle should fill to its rim,
Then I know the memories of me
Are gone from your vision.
If I could go back in time to the days
When we were together,
To the time when our love was
Louder than words.
Now that I see that you're not around,
It's your kisses that I'm missing.

HUNGRY FOR YOU BABY!

I approached you with joy.
Hugging you until you can no longer breathe.
Passing my hands across your body,
Your wet body.
Slowing I kiss you on your cheeks,
And whisper in you ear "I love you, I need you"
And you whisper the same right back.
Quickly I bit your earlobe.
You're moaning my name repeatedly!
I drop to my knees.
"Feed me heavily baby!" I said.
Opening her legs,
I kiss her thighs,
Bending her knees,
I lick her body's wetness out of her.
I can see in her hungry eyes,
She is enjoying my lust and passion.
I can see her hands gripping the bed sheet forcefully,
Asking and begging for I,
A wishful man,
Not to stop.
So then I continued again.
Quickly I jumped you with a satisfaction.
And continue to do my work,
Which you call heavenly magic.
She passes her fingers through my hair.
"My god, baby", You said.
I didn't know you missed me this much!"
She said again.
So then I flipped her around,
And tenderly take her from behind.
Touching her breasts side to side,
Wrapping my arms around her,
Pulling her against me,
Rubbing her body down,
With the wetness from our bodies' sweat.
I take a little look to the clock
On the table,
It said 6:59—(SNAP)

I woke up and it was 7 in the morning.
"DAM! It's just Another Dream!"

FOREVER!

I think of you constantly when I am alone.
I say your name to myself
When you're next to me.
Have you ever loved me?
As much as you loved another?
The way it is?
(Our love!)
The way it feels?
(Our kiss!)
To be able to say from the inside of your soul,
"I love you forever!"
Eye to eye and touch to touch,
Nothing could destroy the one love,
That we both hold for each other.
Even though we know each other for a short time.
I'll tell you the truth,
Sweetheart,
I swear I'll never treat you wrong!
Our eyes meet,
The way our heart race,
Your hands are sweaty,
And you can't stand still.
But when I finally kiss you,
Touch you, and hug you,
You will know that my love is forever.
One day we will travel the stars.
Life is sweet when we're hugging and kissing
Each other.
But this love is a serious affair.
And we may have one disagreement too many,
But you'll still be with me forever.
I refuse to shut you out.
I'll struggle and fight for you against all odds.
I'll drop to my knees and pray to the Lord,
That my love for you is true,
And never be in the dark.
'Cause I need to reach you,
And I need to touch you,
Because you're in my heart forever!

MY OWN REVOLUTION

I woke up this morning hoping for comfort.
Saying to myself, "Please, God, not today."
Feeling the fury when I put my feet down on the floor.
My hands shake with every heartbeat.
My eye filled with anger,
Yelling from the top of my lungs,
"Dam you all, you bastards!"
I want them to witness their own murders.
By looking into the eyes of a killer.
I am, they say,
A Brooklyn- born killer.
'Cause my mother didn't show me discipline,
I am a soldier,
A soldier without morals in
A city where you rarely see a fist fight.
Justice can never know how I feel or felt
'Cause they put me like this.
They made me the mad man that I am.
Seeking and destroying anything and everything
In my rough course.
Now I'm here disadvantaged in a four-wall room.
No windows to see the sunshine in my eyes.
No doors to hear someone knock for my freedom.
No one to talk or hate for my pleasure.
Just myself trapped in a room like if it was a cemetery.
Just myself listening to the dead in my head.

THE QUEEN OF QUEENS

The doors to my heart are open to you,
As well as my compassion and love.
It's hard for a man as myself to tell you,
That I want you by me.
I need you to witness the intense and hunger for life.
And the strong sexual desire,
The sexual desire towards you is uncontrollable.
Come and steal my heart away.
Walk towards me,
For you are beautiful.
Your eyes shine as if you are an angel.
Let me hear your voice,
For your voice
Is sweet and rich.
Let me taste the tongue that makes sexy
Concupiscence words.
Throw me your heart,
'Cause I'll be ready to catch it.
Give me your love,
'Cause I'll put it together with mine.
In my mind, heart and soul,
You are everything a man breathe for.
Let me lay warm and naked next to you,
For we both can kiss one another in bed.
Come here and sit with me,
And tell me how to please you constantly.
You may have had lovers then,
But I can out love them all.
'Cause you are the reason for my magic!
And magic is what I want;
I want to share with you.

FOR SOMEONE IN MY HEAVEN!

I miss your every desirable movement.
I miss you kisses,
As well as your time.
Every picture I kept in my album of you,
I remembered.
Every second, every minute, and hour,
I enjoyed the kisses on my back.
You gave me,
YOU!
My lady of heaven gave me light.
You gave me light when my life was in the dark!
You told me,
"Darkness will never be upped and if life
Was any harder, will you be my map!"
"Yes I'll be the map in your life as well as
The heart in your eyes!" I replied.
Let me love you repeatedly in the heaven of love,
You and I can love each other
In a place where time doesn't exist.
I was born poor in an area of hatred.
But with you,
I'm rich in a place with time doesn't exist.
'Cause you are my angel!
And I am the passion in your lips!
And I could never leave myself of you,
For the only thing that I do right,
Is loving you!

WELCOME HOME

You'll be home soon;
I have to get myself prepared.
You'll be home soon,
Have to get a grip on myself.
I can see you're tired of being alone.
I knew you'd be home with me again.
I've missed you for many years,
And I'll take the time to listen,
And take the time to heal you,
Lord Almighty, I've missed you.
From a dull numb feeling
To a dozen of rose bushes growing
Rapidly.
But home is where you're at now,
With me.
I need to get a grip on myself,
Because you're with me always.
I was getting tired of holding on to my senses.
As I fold my hands as a cup,
Catching your teardrops,
I looked at your eyes,
Your beautiful eyes,
It's like a large pair of mirrors.
The years I cried for your presence.
The years I waited for this day to happen.
My Lord, Jesus. Thank you for waking me up.
Now I see what I wanted to see,
And taste what I wanted to taste.
Her beauty, her wisdom and her love.
O your sweet love,
Such sweet love.
No need for your lovemaking,
Because your kisses on my lips do the job.
All I ask is to love me constantly with compassion,
Not with your body.
With your thoughts and not with your gifts.
You're home now!
And with that I'm always satisfied!

PLAY THAT SWEET SONG AGAIN

Let's go home for I can fulfill your dreams.
Let me know what's on your mind.
I see that you need me as much as I need you!
Put your hands on my head and push me down to my knees.
Let me lick your heart out as a madman that I am.
Say the things I want to hear!
Let me bring you down with me,
So we can love the night away.
Say my name once,
And I'll spread your legs wide.
Pull my hair as you will,
And watch me become harder and harder per every stroke!
Stare into my eyes
And wrap your legs around my waist!
Freaking you, is what you crave from me.
Pass your nails across my back,
And let me soothe you down with my touch.
The promising of your body isn't what I want.
But the commitment of my work is what you long for.
If you ask me to please you,
I will I shall please you with the touch of my hands,
To the touch of my tongue down your back.
I would lick out the word "passion"
Out of you slowly,
And suck to the center of you breast slower!
Come and sit on me and kiss me on my chest.
Let me rub my hands across your thighs
And pull you against me.
Let our sweat spread across the bed,
As much as we will.
For every second, every minute, and for every hour.
I will make you want me more and more.
Knowing that we reached our final second,
You finished by holding my hands
And asking me,
"Can we do it again sweetheart?"
"Of course, babe, of course!" I said.

SOLDIER ON A THRONE

I still remember when I was a child.
And when I was young I remember a man
Sitting on a large throne.
This man looked down at me and said,
"Come here my young child and let me tell
You a story about the Ten Commandments and My life.
And about being strong, crushing the Weak, and the bold, and
the beautiful!"
I was interested to know, so I started walking up
The stairs and sat on the top step to listen.
And He began to speak:
"As I sit on my throne as a soldier,
I reminisced the Ten Commandments that are in My life.
I shall not steal!
I stole things that I needed to get me ahead,
Thousands of dollars, priceless jewels, and time.
Besides when your hungry, you will eat.
Plus I can never forget the hearts of many!
I shall not lie!
Jesus! How sweet that word sounds in my ears!
I've lied to keep myself alive and the lives of others that I love! I've lied
to stop the aches
And pain in my heart that the devil in this world has created.
I shall not dishonor my parents!
It's not my fault if my father didn't show me love, or it's not my fault if
my mother didn't show me the truth about life, my life! It's the kind of
lie that makes people confused or Puzzled about what really happened
between Them. So fuck honor! Because I don't have any but my own.
I shall not commit adultery!
It's been done, and it's been left in the past.
I did what I did, and only God will judge me
For my actions! I did it to get ahead in life.
I was able to get myself information that
I wanted, just to hurt others. Because I knew
Who to strike at. Besides I have enjoyed the
Taste of my victories.
I shall not covet my neighbor's house!
There is nothing that desire me in my neighbor's
Home. But yet! I'll be lying again! I will take

What I want out of life. My neighbor's life or his
Diamonds. Because when I see beauty, I will crave to have it!
I shall not cheat!
O, how sweet. I love to cheat. 'Cause with
Cheating, I've gained power with millions of
People who know me! And gained power in my
World of lust, hate, and sweet revenge!
But then again, I wouldn't call it cheating. I'll call it hustle! Because
Everything you need is based on a hustle! And I will make money by no
Questionable means!
I shall not use God's name in vain!
Jesus fucking Christ! How many times have you
Used God's name in vain? I would always speak
In serious vein. Even though they don't realize
It's being used, they still do it. 'Cause it's a habit!
And yes, a bad habit!
I shall not make an idol of the lord!
I will never pray to an idol, 'cause it's always
Been useless! How do you or we expect a statue
To help us in our dying need? It just doesn't work!
If you take the time to read a bible it will say
"You shall not make for yourself an idol in the Form of anything in
heaven above or on earth Beneath!"
And believe in me and you shall have eternal life!"
So go ahead and go to your lousy fucking idol!
I shall not murder!
I shall waste them at will or I would beat them to Death if I could.
'Cause I don't care who they Are!
I've seen people killed by the government
'Cause of some little bullshit crime!
Believe me!
When I tell you, I don't kill for pleasure, but for
Survival. And it's been years of my last death!
My last clean death!
I shall not hate!
I hate because I been hated by people
Everywhere! I would cut out the tongues of those
Who gossip about me, because I hate them all!
My family, my enemies, my government,
And what the future may hold for me!
I hate because it's a way of life, my life!
And if I was just as a God I will perish you for your crimes against me.

44

I have no mercy or Remorse for them nor their brothers or sister!"
I was surprised to hear so much from him.
He picks me up and says, *"Now that's my true*
Personal Ten Commandments!" He puts me on
His throne and walks away from me.
As he walks away he points at a mirror on the
Wall and says, *"Look into the mirror and you will see the truth about*
yourself!" Then he
Disappeared! I ran towards the mirror and I did
Find the truth! The man on the throne was I in
A much later time! That's why I am what I am!
BOLD! VERY BOLD!

EMERGENCY ROOM

Doors open, doors close.
I can see a child crying!
I don't know why he cries,
But he's getting louder!
I see the nurses bring in slides
To see what's the problem.
'Cause I don't know
(I'm not a doctor)
I can feel the pain in his eyes.
"Please my child! Hold that pain inside!"
I said to myself.
I closed my eyes 'cause I don't or can't
Handle the sight of him crying!
Please, Jesus, help that child!"
The doctors becomes concerned
To find the child's problem.
That child bleeds,
But then again, it stopped.
The nurses talk to him but it's no use.
I see the mother's worries in her eyes.
I never cried before, but I'm crying now!
That child intimidates me!
I can see the terror in his eyes.
My God! I can taste the terror.
I remember myself as a child,
And I remember my falls also,
But I didn't feel the terrorism until now.
I see the child in the long white hallway.
The child needs stitches.
But I don't know
(I'm not a doctor)
Yelling loud, yelling louder!
But it's no use!
The doctor leaves his office with a simple smile.
(He found an answer!)
The doctor speaks, and the nurses listen.
Words per words they listened!
They gave him magic after magic!
"Shhh!" the nurse says to him!

Tone One

"Will this make me all better?"
The child spoke softly back to her.
Slowly and slower the child screams lowered.
The child is getting sleepy and sleepier!
He's asleep now,
Finally asleep!
I felt the pain going, going and gone.
The child is content, so is mama.
No more pain, no more worries and no more
Tears for him or I.
The child sleeps for hours before going home!
By then I'll be home,
Dreaming about the child's victory.
Because he is, and will be, all better!

FOR THE REAL PLAYER

It must have been 2 or 3 o'clock in the morning,
And I'm still thinking about that night,
I was so upset with her.
Teasing me will get you nowhere,
Or teasing him will either!
You have all year,
Or may I say your whole life to
Grow in this world.
I don't need your juvenile fantasy.
(Because I'm deaf to it!)
You have told me useless things,
"I've slept with my best friend or *I enjoy sleeping clothesless"* she says
With a joy on her face.
O, how careless she is,
What such a child she is to me!
You dare to call me a dog or a player!
Yes, I am a dog,
A big dog!
But every dog has a master, and I have mine.
You, you're the one who is a player.
She plays her games, I have witnessed it.
She plays her commitments to people,
But she won't keep them!
But then again we all have gifts within ourselves. And she has hers.
My gift is to write in love and in hate for myself.
And you have your own
(Like teasing men).
"My young childish one!"
That's why teasing me or teasing him will get you nowhere!
And yes I must give her credit,
She is a great mother, and he will grow to be magnificent.
But she can't judge me for being bold!
"So bold," she says.
That's possibly why we went in our own direction!
And yes I will miss the times we spoke and laughed together.
(As the good friends that we were once!)
But it's all-new to me today,
And it will be newer to me tomorrow!
But yet I don't know why I worry for her.

She says that she loves to party!
I'm just afraid that her parties will take her too far!
And I worry when she drinks,
('Cause of her playing!)
My God! Can someone wake her from this evil spell?
Sweetheart, making friend is always easy.
But keeping them is always hard.
Just as it's easy to loose, respect, but its always hard to gain it back.
I will always have respect for you.
But it won't be there forever!
Because that word alone doesn't last forever.

JUST KEEP GOING!

Face me for I can stare at your body,
Kiss me for I can taste your tongue.
Lay yourself next to me for my warmth.
Let me water you down with my love,
And I'll rinse you up with my sexual desires!
Knowing that you're with me is heaven,
Because you are heaven, true heaven.
Hearing your voice is a pleasure to my ears.
But listening to your laughter
Brings excitement to my mind!
Open your legs to me slowly
So I can rub your thighs
With the strokes of my fingertips.
Kissing you with all my amorous feelings
At your inner thigh
So I can brings out the real woman within you!
Gripping my hair towards you makes me
Kiss you gently, very gently.
Let me write out words on your breast with my tongue.
And let me bring the animal out from you by
Gently biting your nipples.
Let me grip your ass and pull you against me on my chair.
Wrap your arms around me
'Cause this ride is ever so sweet.
Spread your legs wide for me
And have your back facing me,
So I can rub your crotch with my fingertips.
For everytime you drop a sweat,
I will love you more.
And for everytime you call my name,
I will love you slower and softer.
My dear sweetheart let me kiss you
From behind on the white wall.
And let me firmly rub your breast up and down
With my touch.
For everytime you breathe in my love,
I would push myself against you!
Let me see your soul boil,
So I know you're in heaven, my heaven.

Tone One

I shall push and pull your body against mine for
You're every call of my name!
You said loudly to me,
"This is pure poetry!
Please don't stop! Just keep going!"
Fortunately I must stop!
But tomorrow is another day.
You will get your chance to ride with my love
Again I answered back, exhausted.

WISHING FROM A STAR

I would wish you a star!
I would wish for you the world.
I would wish happiness and joy.
Wish your life to be the fullest,
And if God allowed me to give my life to you,
So then,
Let it be done!
I'm your friend, companion, and your husband.
As I'm your strength and your every step in a mile.
I've seen you sleep as a child,
Night after night.
As you are beautiful in my eyes.
I would pass my fingers across your hair,
As you sleep!
I would whisper sweet gentle words in your ear!
I would wish for your future to be bright,
And let it be the brightest one!
You are the apple in my eye!
And the breath in my body.
You're the reason for me being alive.
I want to give you everything and more,
Take what I have, my life, my time, my heart, and my soul.
Because it's nothing if I can't share it with you!
You're my lover, my friend, and my wife.
You are my ecstasy and the air in my life.
And you are the best thing that I have ever known!
You have touched my heart with your kindness,
And I thank you everyday.
From the touch of your hands, to the kisses on my lips.
There are thousands of reasons why I love you!
But only one way to express it to you
(A Hug)
A hug can mean hundreds of thousands of ways
And I love you is one of them.
And you can be a proud mother to my first born!
You and I can watch over our child grow to be
Strong and wise.
The child would have a piece of both of us!
Our strong will, our love, and our understanding.

And let the child be as magnificent as you.
These are all the wishes
I would ask from that bright star,
Besides being with you.
I love you!

Chapter 3

BARREL OF A GUN

Tell me how it feels to look up at a barrel of a gun?
Are you scared?
I don't want you to be!
I want you to begin to pray 'cause you're dying.
And get prepared to take your last breath.
I don't need your money or your wife
But your heart in my hands.
I would never steal from you nor lie to you!
But you did both things.
And you did it,
Not once but twice!
The second shot is your first shot!
So then put on your white gown and pray.
Because you fucked up!
I'm going to show you where hell really is!
I want you to understand something.
What I'm going to do is painless!
So don't cry, just pray I tell you.
No one knows we're here.
Yesterday you spoke your bull.
Today you lay across the grass
Looking up the barrel of a gun!
I know your life is flashing before your eyes.
And I also know your lungs are airless.
What's wrong?
Can't breathe?
No where to run or hide!
Five men watching over you,
But four of them were yours.
Now the tables are turned.
You're in a total panic.
GOOD, VERY GOOD!
Begging and pleading will get you nowhere.
I felt your body tense when I cocked my gun back.
Aiming for your head,
For that quiet kill,
And
Saying to you with no smile
"Pay back is a bitch!"

Tone One

And then—BANG! BANG! BANG!
I woke up DAM!
I was fucking dreaming!
I have to get that little prick!

BEATING THE BOSS

You lied to me with your partners!
You said you wouldn't double-cross me.
Well! You fucking did!
You set me up like a guinea pig,
And have the nerve to look at me wordless.
Tried to take my world as a joke with your stupidity!
Knowing that I'll cut you open like a pig.
You continued to play tricks with my mind.
And my people asked me why was I stressed.
I wanted to speak but nothing came out!
Just demands for your kill!
Just demands for your murder!
(In my thoughts!)
I had a city behind me,
Now I have the city in front of me!
Wanting to know why I did,
What I did!
Jesus! Your time has come a long way!
But now you have a problem!
I found out what you've done!
Staring down at you at the baseball field!
You look at me and the worries grow inside you
Like weeds on grass!
"No more two-faces you little fucker, no more!"
I kept saying to myself!
I don't see your partners anymore!
I guess they left you dry and terrified!
The good book says if you live by the sword,
You will die by the sword!
But hey, my dear friend,
I'm not the man, who holds the sword,
But the one who orders the one to hold the sword!
It took me awhile to gain my glory in this
Kingdom!
And you thought it was gone from me!
All you did was made me wake up and be wiser
Than you!
Now get ready to be with the Lord!
Bring yourself to the battlegrounds,

Because I'm not the type to pull the trigger and run anymore!
I'd rather watch you die in my view!
"Look at that boy bleed!"
I remember my friends saying!
No remorse, or no tears for you!
I've never seen a man cry, until I seen a man die.
Every weekend I would sit in my car!
And wonder what I've gained!
Your power, your money, and your fear!
But not your wisdom!
You fucking fool!
You are so lucky,
That God was with you at that time.
But there's always another day!
Another chance to waste you!

OPPORTUNITIES

Sorrow fills my heart greatly!
You can't accept me,
You won't accept me.
But it's okay, I'm okay!
Knowing that I wait for your kiss,
I fear that you won't be satisfied!
With my touch or my words.
I fear that my heart will open up to you,
If you're content with my time or my kisses.
I want my presence to be with you.
But the way you move or speak,
Disturbs every inch of my heart!
I wonder what you thought of me
Or thought of my reasons!
I need you to know the real me!
Because I'm not evil towards you,
But content of your company.
You are my compassion just by your movements.
And you're my deepest vision of a dream.
I'll always be content as your friend,
But then I'm content as your lover!
Honestly!
I can never be content.
I thought of you when I slept.
I also thought of what it may be like,
Your touch, your ecstasy, and your love!
I've missed you so much,
So much when I went away.
Night and day you were in my thoughts.
Night and day you were with me,
In my dreams and in my bed.
But I'm back now for keeps!
Why, O why,
Can't my heart stop hurting?
Why can't you just know me?
The real me?
Maybe it's just me
(Dumb, deaf and blind)
Sweetheart, my sweetheart!

You or I will miss our opportunity!
And I really need that opportunity!

GLADYS VARGAS, MY MAMA!

I've dreamed of mama one night,
And it wasn't a good dream.
I've dreamed of myself
Laying my head on my mother's lap!
And I was crying like a baby!
I constantly kept saying
"Why, mama, why?"
But she couldn't answer me!
She just scratched my head softly.
I've dreamed of someone dying,
But I didn't know whom!
I just wanted this dream to end.
I dropped so much tears, hoping to wake up,
But I couldn't, hoping to know why,
But I wouldn't!
And mama won't speak!
Just short mama with her small grin on her face.
Still hour after hour I cried in my dream.
Because with mama I felt no shame!
And if I could hear her speak
She would say
"Shhh! No mas mi nene! No mas!"
I'm still holding on to mama,
'Cause I didn't want her to leave!
It was just her and I in the kitchen.
The stove was on,
She was cooking.
Still wanting to know who was dying,
Or who died.
I looked inside the pot.
She was making chicken soup!
Mama was cooking just for me.
She stood up and walked towards me,
And hugs me tightly!
And says, *"Te amor mucho!"*
Then I knew the person who died in my dream!
MAMA!
Why mama? I said to myself!
I said "mama" so loudly in my dream,

That I woke myself up!
I woke up still with tears in my eyes,
Tears on my neck.
I felt so much pain within me.
I jumped off the bed and ran
To the payphone outside!
The phone rang once, then twice!
And finally my mama picks up!
And says, *"Hey, what's up, baby?"*
All I can say is "Nothing mama!"
Just wanted to say I love you!"

THE BROOKLYN AMUSEMENT PARK

There were bright lights everywhere.
I just love going to these places.
Popcorn and games, sodas and rides,
The place was huge and astonishing.
There were so many people,
Even children as myself there.
I've walked everywhere,
Sucked on candies and ate hot dogs!
I was having fun!
With the exclusion of that split second!
I witnessed a murder!
All I saw was a man with an extremely large knife.
And he was raising it down to his victim!
They heard the man yelling out
"I'm going to kill you for what you've done!"
This man must have stabbed him about 14 times or more!
(I've lost count!)
There was blood all over the victim's body!
But as a child I stood in shock!
I won't dare to move!
The man just kept going on!
I could clearly see the blade
Going into the victim.
(His Victim)
Everyone in the place was running
Out of there!
(But Me!)
I couldn't move! I was scarred!
What did that victim do to that man?
Why did that man go crazy?
So many questions went through my mind!
He just kept saying loudly,
"WHY! WHY! Why did you do those things to me?"
This man was on his victim for about ten minutes
Before the police arrived.
Then I knew it was over!
The murderer, the victim and my fears!
But for the strangest reason,
I went along my business!

I never looked back,
Or I never knew if the victim lived!
But I do know it was going to be another crazy
Night in Brooklyn for this 7 year old.

NO LOOKING BACK!

It's not the same anymore!
It's not the way it was!
Walking the streets like the rats in my life.
12 years here left me mindless,
12 years there left me unwanted.
But I'm very much grown now!
I've wasted all those years on pleasure!
Now I'm using it on the responsibilities of my life.
From staring down at a dead man,
And being in a jail cell,
To being understanding and compassionate
To those around me.
No more running with my gun cocked,
Or no more drinking with the boys!
Just me!
Full content of what I've become!
I learned the mistakes I've done,
By preventing the mistakes.
I don't worry about losing,
'Cause I'll gain it back again.
I'm not used to it.
(Being alone!)
But it's getting comfortable.
I don't need to look over my shoulder,
But it's always been a habit!
Watching those who died in the past!
I've missed you all,
Even my enemies.
Because you made my veins flow!
"You can take me out of the ghetto,
But no man can remove the ghetto out of me!"
(I used to say!)
It's all gone—my old paradise!
But now! I'm grown! 25 years old grown!
And finally there's no looking back!
I'll just leave it there, far back!
With the skeletons in my closed!

LET'S PLAY

The painful life I live with,
You won't survive.
It was your fault to wake the anger within me.
It was your fault when I spit
At the noise of your name.
Punch me in the chest as you use to!
Slap me when I sleep of heaven!
Things changed, I changed.
It's over with the little brother abuse!
And the end of my embarrassment.
Come across my path,
And play with me.
You'll see I'm not playing anymore!
Punch me in my face,
(Stay silent you asked me!)
Yes! I'm still silent
(I can keep secrets!)
Laying on my bed, still silent,
I wait!
I wait for my time to come!
My anger, my hatred, and my way.
No more love or annoy.
Wanting deep down in my dark heart,
To beat you to death,
But I can't!
The hateful life I live with now,
You won't survive!
It's your fault too hear me curse at you,
With so much meaning behind it!
It's your fault! —I tell you!
I stared up at you,
As you were giants,
I stared down at you now like
Three little pigs.
Looking at a picture of us on the table,
I wipe my hands across the pictures,
As the crumbs on the table that you are.
We must forgive and forget!
(Yes! I agree!)

But to forget is impossible
And to forgive is useless.
Deep in my heart, I would crush you
In my bloodless dream,
And spit at you when I wake!
O, how much I hated you then,
O, how much little care I have of you now!
I learned so much from you!
I stored so much from you!
I wait for your apology.
(It's never acceptable with me!)
Let's play the games when we were young.
The games of punching and kicking!
Today I would win,
And tomorrow you will perish with tears as I did!
As a child I held in my anger.
But as a man I will bring my mountains upon you all!
We were born as a family
(Together)
But who says we must stay together?
Now in the corner of my mind,
Just as my world, I'm alone
(Just me, myself and I)
Alone! And still silent!

TO THE WIVES

A marriage is based on love and understanding.
And not on being jealous and careless!
To be able to write letters with love always in the end,
And not sincerely yours.
To be able to go to sleep after a meaningful apology
Instead of going to bed upset with whom is wrong!
Sharing your thoughts with them is sweet
But spending your time with them is sweeter.
To be able to feel warmth from them when you sleep,
Until they give you a cup of coffee
When you wake!
To be able to say, "I Love You"
For no reason is beautiful,
But to show it from your heart is incredible.
To be able to take care of us
When we're sick or feel well.
To be able to massage
Your feet when you worked hard.
To be able to celebrate
Our anniversary each year...
To be able to give you a flower
For your sweet ways!
With your beauty and my strength,
With your wisdom and my courage,
With your flavor and my touch.
We're the baseball team with the most homeruns!
You're my sunshine
And my only rainbow.
And I'm the strength in your body and voice!
I'm your servant and you're my queen.
You're my advisor and I'm your king.
Together we add life into our years.
Because we are the children in everyone's eyes.
Your my wife and I'm your husband,
And we make things happen!
My dear love,
You are my magnificent and always will be.
So for the behalf of all of the husbands of the world,
I wish you all a great and happy anniversary!

AN ILLUSION

Nothing seems better than making love to you
On the beaches of ecstasy.
And nothing will be better than doing it in the
Middle of a thunderstorm.
Gently kissing you on the lips,
I taste the strong saltwater.
Kneeling down with you,
My shirt comes off slowly.
Kissing you on the neck amorously,
Your blouse drops to the ground.
Passing my nails down your back,
You close your eyes and gently sigh.
Passing my fingers through your hair,
For I can gently bite your chin!
And you speak your sweet words,
And say, *"That feels so nice!"*
No music playing, just the music
Of our heart beating crazy.
Only listening to the rain,
The smell of the ocean water
Makes my body boil.
Not worrying about the sand on our backs,
Because the rain always washes it off.
Having no worries about who is coming,
Because our salted bodies
Makes our blood race!
Closing my eyes I feel the rain
Falling down on my face.
Fall on your back and let me pass
The rainwater downs your chest.
Let me lick the water off your body with my tongue,
And massage your sides with my touch.
Let me whisper secret things in you ear,
And let me hear you gasp for me!
The more it rains,
The more I'll melt by your presence!
The more it thunders,
The more we let our bodies burn!
I looked up and the sky began to lighten,

Tone One

I looked at you and the rain has passed away!
But so did you!
(It's all just an illusion!)
But it's no bother to me!
It was just the perfect dream,
With the perfect woman!

CALL THEM WOMEN

All women create the man today.
They create us by the passion of being warriors to
Survive the world!
Women gave the men something to remember.
As the joyful times in their lives.
They satisfy us with the pats on our backs,
And the kisses on our chests.
They refresh us with love and pain.
They remind us that they love us.
And to show us that we can be equal to any other man!
And with that,
Any other will never undertake us.
Because we're men and they created us!
They fulfill the feelings on our backs,
With their touch.
And the wetness on our faces
When we sweat.
They make us understand our mistakes,
Even when we are successful.
Telling us it's okay to cry,
When we mess up, because they won't tell.
Respecting our thoughts was our greatest victory,
As well as the shines in the sun in our
Darkest moments.
They are the chefs in our bellies,
To the nurse of our ugliest illness.
They tell us that we are number one,
Even when we feel like number two.
We will follow the road you chosen for yourselves,
Because we will protect you
From another who crosses your dream.
To be able to create the best in us.
So we will know that you will always love us.
Because we are men,
And they created the definition of all men.

WHO KILLED CASANOVA?

The middle of winter,
A cold winter.
And there's someone missing.
The neighborhood didn't care of him,
Not even me,
Because I was young.
He was seen on Tuesday
But disappeared by Saturday.
The man they looked for was gentle,
Once said by a woman!
The woman also said he was a gay man,
And a happy one at that.
He was well known
For his kindness towards the women.
I remember someone calling out his name,
"Hey! Casanova! Yo! Casanova!"
It just stood in my mind!
(His lousy name!)
The winter of that year was bad!
The snow covered everything even my knees.
The police didn't find no motives or no answers,
Not even a witness.
'Cause the neighborhood didn't care!
It was just another day of drugs and gambling in Brooklyn.
This gay man the woman spoke of
Was a tall dark fellow with colorful beads around his neck.
And he wore black tight jeans!
She wondered where he was.
My concern was the snow,
Because the snow was keeping the school away!
Late that night I thought of that woman missing Casanova.
I honestly didn't care!
('Cause I'm young)
But soon after the week was over!
The snow was disappearing,
And I went back to school.
Soon after school was over,
The neighborhood began their words and their curiosity.
I guess the police found him.

(Gay Casanova)
I never saw him but I heard of him,
He was dead for about a week!
Covered by cardboard and snow,
The neighborhood still didn't care,
But hey I didn't either.
Cut by an ax,
Which was said and there was still parts missing.
Sitting on my steps I remember the woman Crying for him,
"O, dear Casanova,
Poor woman, she really cared.
But I didn't,
Nor the neighbors.
"Casanova, O- Casanova,
Just another victim done by dealers and Wheelers.
Casanova, O- Casanova,
"A gay man is all he was!"
(My neighbors once said to me.)

NO SUMMIT

Its still daylight and I want you,
To witness the fire within me,
And taste the force of my desire.
Feel my kisses upon your neck,
While my hands wander down your back.
(Beauty and the beast are what we are.)
Dropping to my knees is where you want me,
And licking your belly button is what you call for.
You're the woman I've dreamed of,
Now you're finally mine!
I stared at you the same way you stared at me,
Hungry!
Minute after minute you call for me!
Passing my touch down your legs for I can hear you burst.
Wiping my mouth just as the beast that I am,
You call for me for a kiss.
I grabbed your face and kiss you firmly
With amorous consistent passion.
"Sweet as the mango's in the field of
Puerto Rico is what you are to me. " I said.
You sit in a position I can never forget!
We won't see daylight until one of us gives in.
The harder your breath,
The more I would sweat.
The harder you pull,
The more I kissed your chest.
Making you wet is what I wanted.
Wrap your legs around me
For the strength won't disappear.
You and I together sweats like the waves of the beaches.
Begging and pleading for me "Not to stop"
In the four-wall room,
(Is extremely splendid)
Hour after hour no one gives in,
Time after time we still pushed and pulled!
"Jesus",
We both quit! —No winner, no loser
Just a deep breath, and a smile!

WAITING FOR A PRAYER

If I could wish for love,
The love would be from you.
If I could wish for health,
The health would be given to you from me.
In my sight, my brown-eyed sight,
You are the sun in my morning
And the star in my evening.
Wishing and praying for your breath
Down my Spanish neck.
Longing for your voice.
I stare at myself in your eyes.
Yearning for that gentle kiss,
I wait like a young child
(Actively)
Wishing for your fragrance,
I taste your beauty on my tongue.
You're the woman who I crave for.
If I was a rose,
(Your yellow rose!)
I would spread my scent wildly for you.
If I was a letter,
(Just as this one!)
Read me like the thoughts I've told you.
Hug me and tell me you need me!
And I'll thank the Lord for my prayer.
Blow me a kiss as you used to,
As you always do!
And let me kiss your hands,
As the consort of this prince that you are.
In my sight, my brown-eyed sight.
You are the feeling in my touch,
And the taste on my tongue!
Speak to me as you used to,
As you always do.
Pass your hands across my face,
And say you adore me!
Your presence is the thirst,
Of every glass of water I drink.
And you're the strong hunger my body calls for.

Tone One

Yes! I've missed you!
Yes! I quiver for that wishful hug.
I wait as a young child
(Actively)
I wait for those sweet strong gentle words
"Come and hold my hands, my Spanish Poet!"

BIG WIN

Cold as the hunger of a snake,
But sassy as the suits that you wore!
To be able to crush your dreams
As you did once to me,
Brings joy to my bloodless soul,
And nightmares to your restless sleep.
To call upon your death bed,
Has been sweet to my revenge.
Feel the fury when I slam my hands upon the table,
And taste the victory of my big win.
Have you paranoid when you drop to your knees.
Because my actions are ever so spiteful.
Seeing you suffer as I did once,
Makes me giggle when you cry endlessly.
Cover you face when I beat you,
And close your eyes when I cock my gun.
Remembering when I was there,
You watched over me like a little ugly swine.
You gave me darkness and hell,
And called it home for my own!
Evil as the shades on my face,
But I am strong as a sledgehammer
Breaking through a concrete wall.
"Take away this life!" you, said once.
But my memories will always be there.
Spitting on the ground where my friends died.
I wait for the perfect plot for you.
But to hear that you're in jail, silently!
Has my upcoming happiness.
I've dreamed of your terror!
And the terror of my brothers waking you up!
You will see that my victory was always a big win!
Not for you, but for me!

BRING IN THE RUCKUS!

I've come a long way from hell,
And I've come alone,
To hear you speak.
I've cursed a thousand times
In my thoughts at you.
In my mind,
I have begged for a moment of peace!
Is there a such thing?
I have witness hell in many
Forms and temperatures.
And I'm forced to show it in full bloom.
My dear Lord!
You woke the vengeance unwisely,
Now speak your garbage to the child
that became a man!
A moment of silent,
Is what I demand!
And listen to the mad man
that has a high degree of hate.
You spoke big words to many people,
and brought your army to offend me.
You couldn't let me breathe the fresh air.
Or let me settle down peacefully.
So then!
You spoke your lies,
and tried to make me look small.
You thought wrong of me;
(I didn't care)
Because I remained silent.
There will be no mercy!
None at all.
Because mercy isn't prejudice!
And I was getting prepared
To bring in the ruckus.
Screaming for vengeance
Entered my dreams when I slept.
Screaming for pain went through
My mind when I walked alone.
My maker'll dam me,

And if I had the strength of a God,
You would have seen death
By a stroke of a slap!
I brought in the ruckus
When you were beneath me.
Now I'll bring in the chaos
When I bury you deep under a marked tomb!
Eye for an eye is reasonable for me.
Because you are less than my victims.
But to see the watery eyes of my maker
Makes me realize that life,
Is important to us all.
That is the reason why,
My maker says
"Humanity is everything to me,
So let the swine live painfully!"
I know that we'll meet again,
And my maker won't be their forever!
But until that day I must say to you!
"Leave me or I'll change my mind!"

DAYDREAMING

I was young and curious,
In my very own bedroom.
I would daydream of relaxation,
And pleasant pleasure.
I've dreamed of the Virgin Islands,
Filled with palm trees and mangos.
Thought of swimming in the warm beaches,
With beautiful tropical fishes.
Fantasized dancing with my youth,
Over and over again.
Visualized myself kissing my young puppy love!
(who could forget their first love!)?
Imagined filling myself with life
And harmony Justas like an eagle.
So I can proudly feel the breeze
On a high mountain.
Pictured myself as a turtle,
So I can take my time at life.
Have my shell wrapped around me,
Like a precious quilt of love.
I've dreamed of being a king,
With my beloved wife as my queen.
"Sit next to me my love!" I spoke lightly.
Because my daydream is your reality,
And your reality is my daydream.

WORTH A CENT

Remember me?
My old little man!
I was the young man,
Who you called,
A worthless son of a bitch!
Done your trivial talk of me,
When I was down and
Had my pockets filled with crumbs and lint.
I also remembered you clearly,
When you tapped on a table
With your fingertips.
(Did you know that the table was mine!)?
Ten years has vanished before our eyes,
And God introduced gifts for some of us.
I am seriously amazed that you
Are alive.
(But broke!)
Your lies took you so far,
I guess a wheel came off your
Red wagon of lies.
Because you carried your crumbing
Bullshit on your wagon.
You stopped me in the middle
Of a crowd,
And said, *"You aren't worth a cent!"*
Today I finally speak to you
In front of my company,
Just to say quietly from my heart.
"You are less than a rock!"
I recalled the time when you cursed at me.
And if I had the courage
And confidence within me,
Then.
Today I would definitely have told you,
"I will crush the existence out of
Your spongy saclike lungs!"
But the times have changed me,
And so did the years.
So I'll just accept the fact,

That you will never be better than I.
Because this worthless son of a bitch
Is making pleasant green notes!

A BOY'S ACCEPTANCE

I fantasized dropping to my knees
On the cold bathroom floor.
I covered my eyes with the fist of my hands.
I knew there was a mirror right over me,
I whisper to myself.
Boy: "Mirror, mirror on my wall,
Can you tell me what's wrong with me?"
A few moments later I heard it loud!
A noise of some kind began with a voice,
A deep voice!
Satan: *"O-my dear boy! How stupid can you be?*
You sit on that dirty floor and utter a
Plaintive on your little victory.
But where did it get you? Nooo where!
I remembered you to be spiteful and vicious.
Reckless as my sons and bold as your God!
You use to be angry at life because it spit
You out like a rat. You yelled my name for
A wish, and now you're screaming for power
And glory. I refuse to listen and grant you Anything from me.
Boy: "If you call, covering my eyes a whine!
So then you're stupid! Besides I was thinking
About the victory of passion, and not for
A dam wish from you!"
Satan: *"Victory of Passion? No such thing*
Existed in this century. I personally destroyed
That when I tricked eve into eating that
Sweet red apple! Plus I heard you thinking
Out loud and I understand your problem.
You wish you had a clean life or have the money and power of years
ago!
But you know! it's not happening until
You come to me with open arms and say
My name loudly!" Lucifer!
Boy: "NO! You little bastard! I won't,
Let you drowned my head with nightmares of hates and have you
Wash my body down
With blood and say I caused it!
I've had money and power then,

But my God! The lives I've destroyed to have it.
It serves you right if I choose to reach through this glass and crush your
throat.
Satan: *"Well, well, well! don't we have balls!*
Don't you mean it serves you right if I
choose to reach through this glass and crush
Your throat! You sit on that floor swearing
And damming at me like a prized lunatic.
What are you trying to do? Run for office?
I think not! You are a young little spic
With no real life! No living white trash will
Give a crap, so end this dumb game and
Come with me! Didn't I love you when you asked for it, or didn't I
listen when you cried for vengeance on democracy!
So why the fuss?
Come in man! Come in!"
I stood up to meet him eye to eye and
He began to smile at me.
I shook my head and said
Boy: "Since a young lad, I was called a spic,
A nigger lover, or a motherfucker! I was
Put down with words and rose quickly with
Hatred. Never in my life have I seen you
In my worst or best day! You should know
Me by now that I would have cursed you
Endlessly, so stop your begging and offers.
Because it's not needed here!
And when my first seed is born,
DON'T YOU DARE!
Masquerade yourself to being the father,
The son, and the Holy Ghost! Because I'll
Be part of your dreams and terrorism
Until you crawl back to your abyss!"
Satan: *I know! I've seen your terror and*
Tasted your hate, Jesus I love it!
And to think I was hoping to see you grow
Powerful in my army! But you boy
Fucked up!
I was fed up with his offers and promises.
I couldn't see myself suffering again.
A memory came to me once about a woman saying that satan can't hear
your thoughts.

And I wasn't planing to tell him the real
Truth of my victory of passion!
When it was peace within myself!
No more pain for them
Or I, not even peace,
But only for myself!
I starred deep into the eyes
Of this satan. While reaching for the light
Switch I spoke rashly to him.
Boy: "Cry if you must! but leave me out of it!
Because it makes me a better man and
A bigger man to have acceptance in my blood!
I began laughing with him while walking
Out, all I heard was him yelling.
Satan: *Hey boy! Listen, if you can live with acceptance, try this,*
Peace in this world without grief,
And grief in this world without peace!
You foolish boy!"
He ended the conversation,
Laughing!

Chapter 4

THE TRUTH OF FRIENDSHIP

If I could take back my words,
I would,
(but I can't.)
I'm a hardheaded man
With very harsh words.
I allowed you to speak your nonsense.
But it doesn't influence the problem.
It wasn't about symbolizing erotic desires.
But being truthful to yourself
And our friendship.
I've said many things to you,
Not once was it to sleep with you.
Not once,
Was it to create an affair.
But to see you plush and smile!
You created an insane man out of me,
In your head.
When that insane man don't exist.
You came to me for advice,
And I answered each one patiently!
"Making friends is always easy.
But keeping them is always hard.
Just as it's easy to lose respect,
But it's hard to gain it back."
Jesus! Don't say I've scared you
With my voice of power!
When all it was,
Was your shadows.
Even thou I'm upset with you
I feel ever so foul and despicable.
I've missed those laughers,
And those cheers.
I've basically missed your friendship.
I'm sorry to hear that we're silent,
Cause you mistaken my words and my feelings.
God can only know how many times
I've beaten my head in!
But the words I've spoken to you
Was truly cruel,
But again, true.

Tone One

I'm a man with no shame,
And a man with the need of the truth.
I wish I would bring back the comfort.
But the ire in my pride won't allow it.
If I could bring back those words,
I would,
But I can't!

CLOSING MY EYES!

To touch your heart,
And feel your emotion,
Is what I wanted from you.
To sit by your side
And whisper "sexy!" in your ear,
Is what you wanted from me.
Give me your sunshine,
For strength
And I'll give you rain,
For refreshment.
Tell me your secrets,
And feed me the truth of your desire.
Hold me and never let me go!
Because your company is what I needed!
Pass your nails down my chest
And say you love me!
Alone in my mind as well as in my room,
I thought of you with me
(minute after minute)
And nothing is going to destroy my feelings
For you.
Kiss me with force and bit my lips,
For I can pull your hair and lick your
Neck.
Sit on my bed and wrap your legs
Around my waist.
So I can touch your cheeks
With my fingertips.
Whisper *"Take me now!"* to me!
And open your legs to me.
And watch me bit your inner thighs,
With intense affection and strong fondness.
Remembering only my feelings towards you,
Brings excitement to my eyes.
And screams to your voice.
Viewing every inch of your light skinned
Body
Makes me sweat foolishly
With loyalty.

Tone One

Closing my eyes I can see your beauty
In my thoughts.
And opening my hands I feel your
Body close to mine!
But when I open my eyes
And close my hands
You are no longer there
But your scent! your beautiful scent

WHITE SHEET

Driving at top speed,
I was going insane of this incident.
I couldn't stare at him,
But hope for his survival.
I must have ate six red lights,
To arrive at this hospital.
Holding tightly to my steering wheel
I wouldn't even dare stare at him,
Or his bloody shirt.
Putting in his finger into the deep wound.
Just like the little boy who put his finger
In the crack of the dike,
to stop the flow
Of the water.
My poor loyal friend
Remembering only in that second
When I yelled to him
"Watch your fucking back!"
But he didn't listen,
Now look at that sorry soul.
Deep into his eyes and mine,
I knew he was going!
"Please God don't take him now!"
I played in my mind.
(over and over)
Finally I arrived,
(Finally!)
But in a blink of an eye,
He's on a stretcher.
And I couldn't say a word,
He's through the double doors.
Six nurse and two doctors,
Was on that poor lost soul.
I knew he's fighting for his existence,
And I know the lousy grim reaper
Was watching over him.
Just waiting for the time to touch him!
As he struggles and fights for life
I was hoping and praying for him.

But when our night was over,
He lost that painful ugly fight.
(I knew he was gone!)
DAM!
Holding in my anger was impossible,
I left the hospital.
Holding in my madness
I drove away quietly!
Looking at the passager seat.
I held in the tears at the sight of his blood.
I'll know he'll meet his foes
In heaven or in hell!
And if he could hear me now,
I would say to him!
"Just relax and let yourself go,
Cause I'll know you had problems with God,
Now is the time to patch things up!"
I know deep in my heart
That I should've been there for you!
I felt that bullet more in me,
Than you,
And I was breathing harder,
Than you were.
Jesus! Why couldn't I have that wound?
Thinking of him on that table,
I saw myself closing his eyes.
And I also see the doctor
Covering him with the white sheet!
I knew he was crying!
I knew he was in pain.
But no more tears from him (no more!)
I remember, the war,
And the way he wanted to leave the war!

DYING ENDLESSLY!

Dying to listen to your voice,
That sweet unforgettable voice.
Weeping to see your smile,
On that beautiful face.
I've said what I wanted to say.
(The truth and only the truth!)
But you still keep your distance.
What are you scared of?
Yes!
I'm hurting of you voiding me
Yes! I'm still in pain!
Of your harsh words.
I've enjoyed the glow on your face,
But you're still dull of my ways of expressing.
I've asked you,
Once or twice,
"Do you trust me?
And
Do you believe me?"
And you replied *"Yes"*
Jesus Christ! YES!
But why continue with the cold chill?
I would never hurt you,
Or be demanding to you.
Deep inside of myself.
I've cried endlessly
And moaned loudly for you!
Speaking in my own mind
I've said your name
In my dreams and my nightmares.
(Depressed? Yes I am)
When you pass by my eyes,
I hope for my heart
Not to tumble or crumble.
Call me for I can hear your voice.
Stare at me and give me the look
Of a queen,
Or a young princess
For I miss your presence and your

Tone One

Sweet voice!
Tell me your problems
So I can give you advice
Give back the memories of laughers
And cheers.
And forget the sorrow and the pain.
Bring back the plush and the smiles,
And take back the torments and the cries.
When you speak and say *"HELLO"*
With a numb gray feeling,
I felt it as a stranger I've met
On the ugly streets of Philadelphia.
Jesus! I'm dying with that
Ugly language! (You gave me!)
All I ask, is to come back to my
Heart and soul!

"MISS OPERATOR!"
Dedicated to Barbara Sienko

Who may answer the phone,
When I call?
I won't know,
But there's a lady on this line!
"I've called you and I've asked you!"
"How many times must I take the gossip?
And how many times must I wonder
The fact of whom is gossiping?

Operator*: "Give me your ear and listen to my*
Answer! For it won't be your last!
I'm not your enemy, nor your answer!"

She replied worryless.
Sitting on my chair, patiently
I sit back and listened to this lady.
She began by saying

Operator*: "There's a time to live, and a time to die.*
A time to act real, and a time to be a fake.
But in your life time,
Don't take the fools in your hands,
But witness their down fall!
I have seen you act mature and as a
Child. But never I've heard of you
Forgetting where you're from!"

But I ask you again, I said inpatient
"How many times must I take the gossip?
And how many times must I wonder whom
Speaks of me?
This lady I don't know, takes a deep breath
And begins to speak again!

Operator*: "No one speaks of you or understands*
Your way! For it was I who gossip about
You! Not for harm, but proudness
Not to determine your foulness,

Tone One

But your great fondness!
In this life time or next,
You will be the great and the strong!
For not what you are,
But for what you have become
My Grandson!

NOTHING MOVE BUT THE MONEY!"

There's no need for whining!
Just give the wallet up,
Or your ugly life is gone!
Don't say your bull of,
"I have a wife and kids!"
Cause they're not here.
I said don't cry!
Just give up the gold and cash!
Trust me when I tell you,
I will blow a hole in your gut!
You don't know me at all,
But yet.
We came across a path once or twice.
I've seen you flashing your money,
And I've seen your fancy cars!
Mr. Bigshit is before me,
And I never knew you to cry until now!
Don't offer me drugs or power,
Cause I have it in my hand already
"Its called .45 Automatic"
So lay off the fucking crying!
And give me the loot!
I never enjoyed digging in my pocket,
When it was always empty.
I never enjoyed being rejected
In a job interview.
That's why we'll here so I can eat and live.
I know you can't breathe at this time,
As well as I know your trying to keep
Your tears and life.
Watching me watching you pass the cash
Quickly as possible!
Hearing this man speak one word
(Over and over again!)
DAM! DAM!
Thinking about this man,
I thought
He'll still be positive,
Cause he'll gain it back

Tone One

I just wanted to wet my hands
With money and jewels
(His money and jewels)
But tomorrow,
I'll learn to earn my money,
And tomorrow,
I'll work at a 9 to 5 job!
And possibly I will be able to stay
Existancing in this world!
But right now!
I want the cash or feel a slug in your gut!

NEVER SAYING GOOD-BYE!

I never had the chance,
To say good-bye!
Or I never had a chance,
To fix the mistake I've done.
I'm sorry,
For the first time,
I'm sorry!
Let God beat me with sticks and stones,
Cause I destroyed my chances to heal it.
I allowed you to slip through my fingers,
And what I did was an act of love.
DAM! ME!
For being a fool!
I'll never have the chance,
To say good-bye,
But again I did!
Farewell!
Take care of yourself,
Or
Just a lousy good-bye!
I should have said something
But no! I was much too prideful.
I'm sorry for it, please believe me!
Why can it be the way it was?
I would have jeopardize the world
To bring back the laugher and the smile.
Your friends will miss you,
But I'll be dammed,
Cause I'll miss you the most!
Everyone would be heart broken,
But I'll be torn in two!
I knew I should've said something,
But I couldn't speak or show reaction.
(I knew I was in shock!)
I would have crushed any existence
For your touch!
But the memories I have,
Will still be there!
So will the fragrant of your perfume.

Tone One

I knew you cared for me,
I sensed it.
And so did the world!
(I knew you to void the truth!)
I never had a chance to fix the mistakes I've done.
But I hope you have a chance
To come back to me!
So then, I can say,
GOOD-BYE

WHEREVER YOU ARE!

Rushing out of his home,
With a mug of coffee in his hand.
I knew he was going to work!
He was running late! (So late)
It was Friday -
A sunny Friday!
And he was receiving a check.
This man was proud of life and himself.
Nothing could loose or imperil this
Man's feelings towards it!
He was proud and full of self-respect!
Greeting everyone by their first names.
(He was cool, real cool)
I remembered days when we spoke
And he'll say
"One day I would leave this place
And never turn back! I've saved
My money and I'll soon be leaving!"
I seriously believed him.
He spoke of making money and helping
His people.
But he never mention about his
Bad investment!
Only if you can see him now!
I was shocked about his appearance,
Of 4 years of me knowing him
I couldn't imagine that sight!
He was homeless and jobless!
No more running out of his house
With a cup of coffee!
Cause he didn't have one
Nor a cup.
No more running late for work,
Cause he had no reason to run.
(He was jobless!)
Not worrying about Friday coming
Cause he had no check.
Just nickels and dimes thrown to him.
This man who was living well.

Tone One

Now eats out of trash cans and
Sleeps uncomfortably in the hallways
Of apartment buildings.
Shoots up drugs in his veins
In the trodden tracks of my house,
And wastes his nickel and dime money on Cheap corn liquor.
I don't need anyone to tell me
That his life was kissed away
(I know! I knew it would be!)
No more riding his fancy car,
Cause he has no where to go!
Mentioning his goals and life to me.
Only broke my heart to see him now!
Dirty, smelling man with no life,
Makes me disappointed to see him now!
I just believed that he just took
Life for the funnies,
And not seriously
And remember I'll miss you
My dear friend,
Wherever you are!

TELL ME YOUR DESIRES!

Tell me how you need to be kissed,
And tell me how should I hug you.
Tell me how to shower you with your favorite
Roses!
And rinse you down with my kindness.
Let me pass my fingers through your hair,
And tell you how sexy you are to me!
Have me fulfill your deepest dream,
And continue with my compassionate
Offering.
Waiting to hear your voice and say *"HELLO"*
Brings smiles to my face everyday.
Tell me the truth about your feelings
Towards me,
And I'll tell you how beautiful you are!
Tell me no one has adored you this much,
And I'll tell you that no one will.
Call for me and I'll be there to listen,
Is as easy as you blowing me a kiss,
Cause I'll blow one back to you.
Tell me your secret desires,
And I'll promise to fulfill those desires.
Relax your head on my chest
And listen to the wood cracking
By the fireplace.
Because it's the heat of my heart
That you feel against your face.
Listen to my heart on this poetry,
And I'll be hoping that your eyes
Will light up.
Hearing to your voice is like starring
To the sky and looking at fireworks
On the 4th of July!
Tell me *"YES I've thought of you!"*
And I'll tell you how much your name
Went through my mind.
Basically tell me your secret desires
And I'll promise to fulfill your desires.

REMINISCING ON IRISH HARRY

"Hey mister! Do you know me?
I believe you don't! I come from
A long line of strong powerful men,
So I advice you to stop and shut up!"
This man looks at me and chuckled,
He starts pointing at me and says
"I worked my whole life and never
Beg for a cent! I started with nothing,
And lived my life as a gang-banger
As yourself, so don't tell me that
I don't know you! Because I do!"
I starred at this Irish red-faced man.
And wonder, what the hell does
He knows?
He spoke hard at me with his green
Jacket on. I saw his hands and he
Did at one time work hard.
He spoke of what gang bangers really
Was like then!
No pistols but your bare hands,
No gambling with money,
But hustling with your knowledge!
True gang-bangers, then, fought
For respect,
And not for a cheap drug corner!
I started giggling at this poor man,
And he stopped my giggling and says.
"I understand when you say I don't
Know you because I'm from the old
School days! But yet I do!
I've tasted those desires of
Money, women, and power.
But in your days now, it's called
Murder and just plain murder!
What you need to do is use your
Talent and go to school.
Learn about yourself,
Learn about life at the other side
Of the fence! Keep hold of what

You earned and use it like your
Wisdom on the streets!"
This Irishman just kept on going with
His story! And do you believe, that
I was no longer giggling!
I said, "Fine then! what do you
Look forward to! A lousy apology!
NO! I refuse to give you one
You spoke your crazy ass days
Of gangster's paradise but hey!
It's the days of who is killing who?
And not about who is hustling who?
But believe me old man when I tell
You, I am impressed with your past
And present!"
He reached for a cup of coffee that
He had left on his table and takes a
Little sip. He closed his eyes and
Hums and says, *"That's good coffee!"*
Then looks at me and finished his
Story with
"I know your impressed with my
Life but don't be! Because I need
You to understand that YES!
I don't know you!
And YES! It was my past,
But you and I are the present
And tomorrow will be your future,
So fix it now then later!"
This man puts his coffee down
And pats me on the back and says
"Come on son, we have work to do on
Your days to come!"

DEAF AND BLIND

I never felt so warm until I met you.
You made me realize that I was important.
You spoke of sharing and thinking with
Each other,
And I thought of spending and hugging
With each other.
Stand!
As a queen should pose.
I starred deep into the glory of your heart.
And I knew that my love is greater
Than life itself for you.
The magic you give,
Is the sunshine in your smile.
And the magic of your marvelous presence,
Makes me crumble as the sandcastles
Made in the beaches of Puerto Rico!
Holding your hands to my chest I asked
"What's in your heart and soul?"
If I had one day to express,
I would tell you a thousand things.
I would ask you to hold me tightly,
And never let me go!
Closing my eyes,
Holding back my wishful tears,
You asked me gently with a whisper!
"Why did it take me this long to notice
Your emotions for me?
"Because passion is deaf and blind,
And so are you!" I answered.
O-my dear grateful God!
Now that you see me in a different level,
I hope you understand me now
And the magic I held in for you!
I thought to myself!
I would pull the sun down to you
Just to fill your darkest evening.
And your heart is more delightful
Than old wine itself.
Let me be your knight in shine armor,

And drive you away on my heavenly glory
Seeken.
Let me strengthen you with my kisses
And refresh you with my touch.
Let me wrap my arms around you
And embraces you tightly!
Let me wake and arouse your love
If so desire.
Show me your face;
Let me hear your voice.
For your voice is pleasant and your face
Is lovely
"Are you faint with love?" I said,
With an enchantment of her presence.
Starring at me with your contentful eyes,
You speak and say
"I'm a rose to you! a beautiful lily in your island!"

MY MISTAKES!

I thought of all the ways to please you,
And thought of all the things I've done.
Tell me what would it take to have
You subside yourself down with me.
All I had was unnecessary pain!
You said *"Your always adored me!"*
(O-Jesus I waited for that dream!)
Standing by a street corner,
I waited.
I waited for my amor to arrive with love,
And at night when I slept,
I dreamed of us in a black and white
Movie.
But my love was in pure color-as always!
You play your love like bushes of roses,
You give me bloom than it died before my eyes.
And if you looked at my life,
Your see,
What I see!
My unnecessary pain!
I guess I needed to live my life
Without you!
And life can only be what I make of it,
Alone!
Jesus! my life is alone!
Closing my eyes,
I can only hope for comfort.
Holding in my tears,
I can only hope
For you to wipe my tears with the touch,
Of your fingertips!
Having your shirt in my hands,
I can still smell the perfume on it.
Dropping to my knees,
I wait for my prayers to be answered!
(I'm a patient man!)
Yelling your name,
I weep for you,
Lying on my bed,

I waited for you!
But you're still not here with me!
Not even a lousy phone call from you.
What have I done to deserve this?
I tried to shower you with love,
But love isn't enough!
I tried to call you calmly!
But you won't let your hands out your ears.
Forget me!
When I actually meant
Or
What I actually wanted to say, was,
Forget me not!

FORGOTTEN YOUR NAME

Two nights of torment,
Two nights of watching me crumble to dust.
Regretting the moments I've spoke,
When I should have listened.
Beat myself when I was unsuccessful,
To the day I can no longer continue.
I've given you my hand to hold,
You have given only memories to me!
(Memories I shouldn't remember!)
Point out my badly mistakes
And maybe I may wake up
From this evil spell.
With so many mistakes I've done,
I see my knees can no longer
Hold the weight.
I dropped to my knees forcefully!
The pain, the cry, and my stupidity
Spreads like blood on my floor!
Blow your kissed to me,
Just as you did to him!
I've given you my every heart beat,
And you laughed at my feelings, my words
And at my sorrow.
These two nights was terror to my eyes.
Only if I could speak the lies,
Would you have listened to my reasons?
NO!
I refuse to speak in that tongue!
But offer the truth of my soul to you.
You covered your eyes to void the truth,
And covered it with your childish play.
My dear sweetheart!
I won't cry any longer for you,
But I will tell you another mistake!
Farewell!
I once knew you,
And today I have forgotten your name!

OVER AND OVER AGAIN

You're the sunshine and the rain,
And you fill me with your hugs and your kisses.
Walk with me and hold my hand softly,
And speak to me with words
Of love and passion,
Let's stand in between shadows,
And let me secretly steal your heart away!
Kiss me on my lips and say I'm special.
So I can lower myself to my knees,
And lay my head on your belly.
Give me your attractive skin toned body,
For I can satisfy you with my touch,
Words and compassion.
Say you love my ways of being careful.
And I'll say no one will care for you more.
Let me inhale the scent of your body!
So I can have you exhale constantly
When I lick below your belly button.
Fulfill me with your compassion
And wetness,
And say you enjoy my touch and my time.
Sit by me so I can hold your hands,
And tell you "Your Sexy!"
Over and over again.
Fill me with an offer that makes me smile,
And I'll speak about you living large
And speaking larger with me!
Be the ink in the pen that I write,
So I can continue telling you that you
Look marvelous sitting on the bench,
Under the moonlight.
I've enjoyed the warmth that you given me
Because you're the sun in my darkest path.
And when you leave my bed
And go back home,
Dream of this
And me!
For your fairy tale can come true!
— Over and over again!

THE GAME IS OVER

The devotion of your tears,
And your love was never forgotten,
Still brings back the memories of you and I.
My palms still sweat with every heartbeat.
Don't stare at me,
For I am hideous inside and out.
Or!
Don't content me with a memory,
"I knew you once for being a strong
Man, a soldier, and a lover!
When actually the man still lives,
And the soldier sleeps comfortably,
But the lover is still in full bloom.
Don't bring back the feelings
I've had once for you!
Because of your heart breaking presence.
I would have destroyed myself
With words of strong ugly annoy!
We must always regret,
What we remember that last,
Two nights of three hours!
We definably enjoyed our victories
Upon each other.
But hey sweetheart!
It's over,
This game is over.
And the devotion of my tears,
And my love was never forgotten!
Still brings back the memory
We had once!
And perhaps it will still remain
A memory that will always be remembered.

DEAD MAN STILL FIGHTING

I'm a dead man,
And I can't wake up!
I opened my tired heavy eyes,
And can't remember what happen to me!
Laying on this cold stretcher,
I can't listen to myself scream.
Who in the world are these people?
These doctors and those nurses
Moving slowly on me!
My God!
Am I dying?
(It can't be!)
Is it my time to go?
Well, I refuse to go without a fight!
And I know I'm not the type to lose easily.
I feel my eyes getting heavier on me,
And becoming weak by the second.
I hope I know that I'm dreaming.
Because I can't hear myself or them,
Or
I can't move one inch of my body!
Forcing my eyes to stay awake,
But it's impossible!
Watching these medical people speak
Over me!
Please! Can't you hear me?
Tell me what's going on with me?
I closed my eyes for a minute,
And I finally heard the angels call for me!
And I finally could hear the E.K.G. machine
Stop reading my heart beat!
"NO! WAKE THE FUCK UP"
I heard the doctor yell
"CLEAR!"
Than
"BOOM!"
The defibrillator gave me life again!
(Thank you lord!)
I opened my eyes

Tone One

And found myself still starring
At the E.K.G. machine
My poor body was still fighting
For a touch of air!
Man! Please wake up!
I felt my eyes going again
Shit! I'm a dead man
And I can't wake up!
I thought about that
Over and over!
In my despicable dream.
Struggle and fought for air and life.
Trying to get up but couldn't
O-my God I'm tired of fighting
For my soul or was it my life.
(I don't know until I go!)
And by chance I woke up!
By my alarm clock.
(Thanks babe you set it for me!)
But hey I know that natural won't
Or
May I say?
Wish natural won't take me yet!

PURE HARMONY

Touch my chest with your soft hands.
Feel the taut from my soul,
And hear what my heart sings.
Let us tell each other our promises,
For we won't make any mistakes,
In our future.
In time we have learned
That we were born for each other
(Just as us being soul mates)
And we shall die for each other.
I see clearly the core of your wonderful
Spirit.
And I feel the fulfillment of your
Intense affection,
And the warm feelings towards me!
I'm overwhelmed by your looks,
Just as your superior force of your body
Calling my own.
Moan and sing your heart out for me,
While we make love on my rugged floor.
Deep and great distance from my own time,
I've never had women as you
Love me this much.
But as always it's pure harmony,
And pure melody.
Wetting my lips with your tongue,
Brings Goosebumps down my back,
And music to your beautiful brown eyes.
You are more than my mate,
But my prey and I'm your hunter.
Conquering is what you desire of me,
But to be able to control the volume
Of your voice is remarkably sweet.
Bring down the moon and the brightest star
In my darkest glorious night.
Because you are the light in my ugliest
Unsightly dream.
You content me over and over again
With your nails down my back,

Tone One

And say that you love my ways
Of overcoming your body, soul, and
Mind.
Because no one will take your place
In my body, soul, and mind.

FROM RAGS TO SILK

Don't stare at me,
Or laugh about my reasons.
Understand my life
And my ways of living.
I have no future for you,
But for myself!
Don't give me cheap hugs or unpleasant kisses,
Because I'm under educated.
(But then again I never was!)
See me as a roll model?
"I don't think so!"
Bless me because I've survived,
Then kill me because I've lived too long.
Point your sinful fingers at me,
And see me shed with no tear.
Walk out of my life,
Just as my daddy did once.
Taunt me to death
With your hideous lousy haunting.
Spit on my shirt and my shoes,
And call me stupid.
Laugh at me when I fall on my face
And witness my will of rising.
Don't cry for my assistance,
Because I'm no longer helping.
Share your thoughts with me,
I don't care to listen.
Say *"I'm proud of you!"* to my face
Then call me a thief behind my back.
Walk into my life,
And feel the coldness in
Me!
The times have changed me
Because I've grown mentally
I've become more educated,
And became less reasonable.
I've accomplished my greatest goals,
And left you all to rot.
Use to call me a mama-boy

Tone One

When I was young.
Now get upset because the women
Adore my presence!
Never could I have written
A summer breeze note.
Now I write strong thunderstorm poetries.
You giggled at me when I was shy,
Now you're walloped by my boldness.
Chuckled at my wedding day
And say it will never last.
But six years has passed us by
And you still looking for that right one.
Basically don't stare at me at night
Or greet me in the morning
(It's not needed!)
Because yesterday I was nothing,
And today I'm more than something.

THE SCULPTURE

Soothe me from my head to my toes.
Tell me that you longed for me,
Since our last encounter.
Wet my chest with your sweat,
And today we will make memories.
Playing my games on your neck.
With my tongue,
(That you call marvelous!)
Is tasteful.
Crest me with your warmth,
From your sinless body!
(O-Jesus!)
Kissing you continually is important
To me,
As myself drowning you with
Rose pedals on my bed.
Let me be the sculpture in your life,
As I'll be able to make a new woman
Out of you when you work hard on me!
You have fulfilled me with kindness,
And promised it for purity and eternally.
Be the earth beneath me,
And I'll be the sun above you.
Be the tree for my shade,
And I'll be the rain when you yearn
For thirst,
Touch my face softly,
And whisper in my ear that you desire
Me for a million years.
Relax your head on my chest
And cover me with the silk bed sheet.
Listen to the voice from my lips
And hear my promises of my commitment.
Is my desire is what you call for?
So then,
My ways of having you relieve
Your body to me will be pleasing to
My hands!
You are my sculpture today and forever,

Because you are the art work for the
Next million years.

REST IN PEACE

Tired!
It felt like months I've had no rest.
What I would give for one night,
Of relaxation.
I thought of starring at my bed,
I wish I could sleep forever.
I dreamed of a coffin,
I needed to slow down.
Now I know what it means of saying
"Rest in Peace!" to the dead!
To be able to sleep eternally
With no living soul bothering them.
To be able to rest in peace in a dark coffin.
And have a tombstone over them.
Who knows death better than I do?
I don't want to die!
But then,
No need to live!
But in my such lively world
The phone rings for me!
I don't or refuse to pick it up!
But I have to.
(It may be important)
I've worked hard so far!
And bought what few men don't have.
But I can't buy sleep or a day-off.
Tired of hearing to their request,
And tired of listening to their mouths chatter.
Give me some rest,
And I may give you some peace.
It's late now,
So late,
I'm finally asleep.
But I'm getting up in four hours.
I need to build a home,
For my beautiful beloved.
And need to build a vehicle for my feet,
Because it'll go so far!
Will I ever rest in peace?

Or be bothered for the rest of my life?
I don't know!
But right now! I am going to sleep!
Good night!

PROUD PUERTO RICAN

Stand with me,
When I accomplish my goals
And succeed in reaching for my dreams.
Be proud of me,
When I offer a hand to my brothers
And sisters,
As well when I mention our color to racism.
You wrapped your love around my people,
And pleased us with the tone of our skin.
Fulfill me with the melody and harmony.
Of being a Puerto Rican.
Everyone asked me,
What is our fuel for passion?
It's the strong yearning for freedom,
That we all feel when we stand
Together as Puerto Ricans!
Dear mama! Dear mama!
Wrap your arms around me,
Like a high cost blanket of pride.
And tell me you're proud of what
I've become for my people!
I know you are,
I am too!
God has filled us greatly with happiness.
But to see my nation and my people
Graded for their ways of living,
Breaks my heart painfully.
Closed us out from freedom,
Because we were tried as uneducated,
But as a educated nation
We asked for only justice.
So I'll ask you!
Would you breathe for me?
If I couldn't live?
Would you stand for me?
If I couldn't walk?
Because I would drink for you,
When you're not able to swallow.
And I would see for you,

Tone One

When you're blind to see glory!
Because I'm a proud Puerto Rican!

To The Reader

Growing up wasn't easy, but it wasn't hard. Mama just wanted me to be okay with my brothers, sisters and myself. When mama found out that I could draw, she asked me to become an artist. And when she found out that I was talented with my hands, like fixing things she asked me to open a contracting business. All I wanted was to be okay with myself. I don't need fame because fortune would be enough. I was just one of those kids who could a bad turn in life. But hey, I fixing it to this very day. And the people I've met in my life just heard me, but didn't listen. If people just took the time to listen to our problems, there wouldn't be problems with us today. I still remember a morning when I ran home to my mama and said "I think I killed someone!" You couldn't imagine the look she pulled out at me. Her 12-year-old son, killing an old classmate! I'm just glad that he lived! because it was a mistake. But back to my story, all I asked was for a little respect from everyone. I worked hard to get here, just as those who thinks highly of me. All I'm basically saying is to be yourself and to your mother eyes. Be a nurse like the great ones I know or the doctor in the family, so you can help take care of those in need. Be a contractor or that special artist and build the homeless a strong home. Be the teacher who you loved the must, or that strong parent who touched your heart greatly. I basically taught myself and that's enough for me. It's not about whom is smarter or richer, it's about who is ahead of the class and how long can you stay there. Because from my view, only the strong can survive. I still feel the same way as I did then, "Step on them or they will step on you!" By all means necessary. Only when I'm pissed off of course! But in my joyful times I'm the lion who sleeps, and the child in God's eyes. People used to tell me that two wrongs doesn't make a right! But hey it does work when your prayers aren't answered. My ladies and gentlemen, I don't need you to gossip about me. Cause its still going on with my family. Or I don't need a spotlight to determine who is the bad guy; I know who I am. Because we all have our own hell and it's killing me everyday thinking about mine. If only I could go back in time where I started it all I would, but I'm not God. And I'm living my life just as you, one day at a time. And for those who cared for me then and now, I love you all dearly. I wrote this letter and the poetry to all those who I love and all that I hate. Because you did listen to me or you just thought less of me for my ways of living and dying. So thank you for listening to my confessions and my cries at night.

About the Author

I was born in Brooklyn, N.Y. and lived in the Bushwick area. Where there I've learned about real survival. Growing up, I was the type to learn why things are the way they are. For example, why are there so many killings? Or why is there so much hate? I've done some crazy things as a child. I use to sneak in the train station and ride on the train cars. Or play hide and seek inside abandoned buildings. I never respected my elders. My friends and I use to steal fruits from the sidewalk stands at the Chinese stores, It was fun then. I lived in a nice size apartment with the entire family; there was five of us, plus mom of course. My oldest sister is a lawyer in Philadelphia, P.A. (God bless her talent!). Second is my brother who lives in Pampano beach, FL. He left Brooklyn due to major problems. Third is my sister who works for a large contracting company in New York City, "my short electrician sister". She finally found something she wanted to do! I left Brooklyn also for major problems. And finally my young brother, he'll probably grow up to be an important person in this family. As well as a handsome young man. I just hope he doesn't take any bad turns as I did! My mother, who is tough but sweet, learned so much in your time. She had my oldest sister at sixteen in Puerto Rico, and was forced to quit school. She educated herself through her mistake and us. She is and will be a mother and a father to us always. When we did wrong, she would kick our butts until we understood our mistakes. (I was hard headed, it took me too long to understand). In Philadelphia I was hooked up with many groups, I didn't need to show any loyalty to them, cause I was snagged. I showed no remorse for my actions! I stole and sold drugs with them and smoked and drank with them. But relax people, I've calmed down plenty. I quit school at a young age and went to find some work for myself. School wasn't for me, but when I was in school I met a real beauty, my wife, although we hated each other in the beginning. Soon after I left Philadelphia and moved to Florida, I began to miss her, and came back to find her. And I did, I asked her to marry me and since that day, we've been together. It was my wife who changed me, and forces me to get my G.E.D. in Job Corps. And left the gangbanger's life alone. Thanks babe! I owe you one! So today I sit back and reminisce the tricks I've done to get here. You can take me out of the ghetto but no man can take the ghetto out of me.

Peace and love!

Tone One